TONY ROBINSON'S

WEIRD WORLD OF WONDERS

BRITISH

Illustrated by
Del Thorpe

KT-376-502

MACMILLAN CHILDREN'S BOOKS

Jessica Cobb is my researcher. This means she does all the work on the book while I jet off to the West Indies, drink delicious non-alcoholic cocktails full of exotic fruit and pieces of coconut carved into the shape of hummingbirds, dance till dawn to the sound of a thousand guitars and sleep till noon in a bed the size of an Olympic swimming pool. Thanks, Jess

Sol Hobbs has known Nits all his life. When his family got her from the dogs' home, they called her Jessie Tat, then when she came to our house we called her Winnie. But Sol reminded us that her nickname had always been Nits, and we've called her that ever since. This book's for you, Sol. Thanks, mate

First published 2012 by Macmillan Children's Books
a division of Macmillan Publishers Limited
20 New Wharf Road, London N1 9RR
Basingstoke and Oxford
Associated companies throughout the world
www.panmacmillan.com

ISBN 978-0-330-53426-0

Text copyright © Tony Robinson 2012
Illustrations copyright © Del Thorpe 2012

The right of Tony Robinson and Del Thorpe to be identified as the
author and illustrator of this work has been asserted by them in accordance
with the Copyright, Designs and Patents Act 1988.

1 3 5 7 9 8 6 4 2

A CIP catalogue record for this book is available from
the British Library.

Typeset by Dan Newman/Perfect Bound Ltd
Printed and bound by CPI Group (UK) Ltd, Croydon CR0 4YY

Hi! We're the Curiosity Crew. You'll spot us hanging about in this book checking stuff out.

This is the story of how one tiny country ended up in charge of most of the world . . . and then lost it all again!

We'll tell you about spectacular naval battles, bonkers inventions and big moustaches. Read on to find out . . .

4

PAINTING THE WORLD PINK

OK – so Great Britain may only look like a little pimple on the face of the Earth to a flying saucer full of aliens, but just over 100 years ago it was the greatest superpower the world had ever seen. It ruled more than 400 million people across five continents!

You'd have had no trouble at all spotting the British Empire in those days, even from outer space. More than a quarter of the world belonged to Britain, and on coloured maps it was painted pink.

No it wasn't. Look – it's black and white.

OK!

Go and have a look at the back cover of the book, silly!

Originally the plan had been to paint the British Empire red, the colour of the uniforms of the British Army. But the mapmakers complained that red was too dark to be able to read the names of the countries written on top of it. So they chose pink instead.

People used to say that '*the sun never sets on the British Empire*', because it was so big the sun was always shining on at least one part of it. From high mountains to flat coral islands, from chilly lands full of penguins to deserts chock-full of camels, the British ran it all!

Today one out of every four people in the world still speaks English, because they live in countries that were once part of the British Empire. The Brits gave them their laws, their daft sports like cricket and rugby, their boiled eggs with soldiers for breakfast, and their scones and strawberry jam for tea.

What's our country called, gang? Why do we pin GB on our athletes, but put UK on our websites?

It's because its name has changed over the centuries . . .

The Greeks called it 'The British Isles' thousands of years ago because it was where the Britons lived.

Originally the biggest island, Great Britain, was three separate countries – England, Scotland and Wales. Then they united together under one king.

Now we're called the United Kingdom of Great Britain and Northern Ireland. This is a right mouthful, so lots of people say Britain or Great Britain instead, because it's shorter. But not accurate.

Have you got that? OK, good!

DOG-HEADED MEN

So how did little pimple Britain get such a huge Empire?

Before the British Empire existed, maps of the world didn't tell you much. They showed the countries that sailors had visited, like Europe, Asia, and the top bit of Africa. But what lay beyond them was anyone's guess! So the mapmakers filled the rest of the world in with oceans full of sea-monsters, shipwrecks and tsunami-type waves, and countries inhabited by dragons and crazy dog-headed men.

Exploring the world's unknown bits would have been really scary. Even if you didn't get shipwrecked or burned to bits by dragons, how would you have known which direction to go in or how long your journey would take?

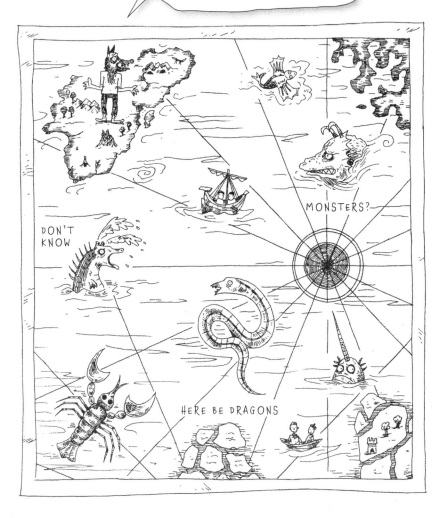

Anyone brave enough to get on a boat and set off over the horizon had to hope that, before their food ran out, they'd reach another bit of land (preferably somewhere where the people didn't have wet noses, and didn't want you to throw sticks for them to chase). You'd have to be daft to take the risk, wouldn't you? And yet once big, strong ships had been invented, people started sailing all over the globe, even though their journeys were often sheer hell.

BLEEURGH!

The Portuguese explorer Ferdinand Magellan spent over three months at sea without fresh food. His crew had to eat sawdust, bits of oxhide, and stale biscuits full of worms and soaked in rats' wee!

I don't know about you, but I think I'd rather have stayed at home playing Grand Theft Horse 'n' Cart, or whatever it was they played in those days.

What on earth was it that made people go through all these horrors? Were they insane?!

Did they do it for a dare?

Were they bored?

No, they had a very special reason. They were all looking for something extremely valuable . . .

GOLD!

The Kings and Queens of Europe loved gold! They couldn't get enough of it; which, if you think about it, is actually a bit weird. I mean, what's so special about gold?

You can't cut it up and put it in a sandwich, you can't build a block of flats with it, you can't set fire to it when you're feeling a bit chilly, and you can't make a decent weapon or tool out of it (swords made of gold tend to crumple up if you try and poke anyone with them, and a golden hammer is about as useful as a chocolate hot-water bottle!).

But kings and queens liked the way gold sparkled. They used it to make coins, they put it in their crowns, they turned it into jewellery, and they bought things with it, like iron (which, unlike gold, is a very good metal for poking people with).

THE ISLAND OF ENDLESS GOLD!

In the thirteenth century a Number One bestseller hit the bookshelves of Europe. It was called *The Book of the Marvels of the World*, and it was all about the adventures of a real-life explorer called Marco Polo.

Starting at the age of seventeen he'd spent twenty-four years travelling to places like China, India, Japan and Sri Lanka. He described his epic journeys on horseback, riding through deserts and over mountains to strange places dripping with silk, spices, ivory and lots and lots of . . .

GOLD!

He said people in the East had so much of the stuff that, if you saw it, you wouldn't be able to believe your eyes! He said there was an island called Cipangu where the amounts of it were endless; the king lived in a palace made of . . .

The floors were . . .

Even the windows were . . .

Back in Europe, lots of people read Marco Polo's book, and thought to themselves, 'Imagine what you could do with all that . . .'

Some of the stories were sort of true – this is the Golden Palace of Amritsar in India. Yes, it's all shiny and yellow (although it's actually covered in thin gold leaf, not made of solid GOLD!!!).

17

So explorers were sent off to find a sea-route to the East in order to bring fabulous riches back by the boatload. But sailing east was harder than it sounds. The route was long and complicated, it was incredibly difficult to work out how to get there, and in the process explorers kept bumping into islands, coastlines and continents they never knew existed! And what did they do when they landed on them? They stuck a flag in the sand, and claimed them for their own country back home.

CRAZY COLUMBUS

One of these explorers was an Italian called Christopher Columbus. He'd read Marco Polo's book and was desperate to be the first person to find a route to the East. He came up with a weird plan – instead of sailing east, he'd sail in the opposite direction and head west.

This wasn't actually as crazy as it sounds. Columbus knew the world was round and that if you travel west, you eventually come full circle and end up in the East.

But it took a long time to persuade anybody to give him the money to try it out. He asked all the Kings and Queens of Europe but most of them thought he was mad.

Eventually, though, the King and Queen of Spain agreed to pay for his trip, and in 1492 Columbus headed off into the unknown. After five weeks of sailing west and seeing nothing but mouldy bits of seaweed and the odd hungry shark, his crew finally spotted land.

But it wasn't the East they'd found, it was South America.

In other words, one of the most famous discoveries in history was actually a complete fluke!

Luckily for Columbus, South America turned out to be full of gold! So he stuck his flag in the sand, and claimed it for the Spanish, who sent out lots of men and boats to dig gold up and bring it back to Spain.

ONCE A PIRATE...

The Brits were really slow off the mark in this whole discovering-gold-and-foreign-countries lark. But eventually they realized they were losing out and decided they wanted a slice of gold pie too. Trouble was, everywhere they went, the Spanish had got there first! There was only one thing to do . . . rob the Spanish!

British sailors became really good at it. Lots of them got extremely rich. One of the most famous was Francis Drake. He sailed all round the world plundering Spanish ports, attacking Spanish ships and carrying off boatloads of Spanish gold, half of which he kept for himself, and the other half of which he gave to the Queen of England, Elizabeth I.

She was so pleased with all this lovely shiny gold stuff that she gave him a knighthood and made him Sir Francis Drake.

The Spanish were furious! They called Drake 'the Dragon', and the King of Spain offered 20,000 ducats (or four million pounds) to anyone who could find him and kill him! But nobody ever managed it and Drake kept on bringing home shiploads of . . .

Eventually the Spanish King got so annoyed that in 1588 he sent a fleet of ships (known as the Armada) to attack England. But the English defeated the Spaniards, and Drake, who was one of the English commanders, left the rest of his fleet behind and sailed off to steal a load of gold from the boat that was carrying all the Spanish sailors' wages . . . Well, he was a pirate!

A 'NEW' ENGLAND

Eventually, after years of fighting, England and Spain made peace, which meant the English weren't allowed to rob Spanish ships any more.

From now on, the English had to get their gold another way. They came up with a brilliant but simple plan . . . They'd 'bagsy' their own bit of America.

In December 1606, three small ships set sail from London. On board were over 150 men and boys who were planning to look for gold in North America, just as the Spanish had in South America.

They landed at a place on the east coast which they renamed 'New England', and set up a little town which they called 'Jamestown' . . .

Is that because we're all called James?

No – they named it after the new King of England, James I.

THE GIRL WHO LIKED TO PLAY

Unfortunately, despite lots of searching, the settlers didn't find any gold. What they found instead were hundreds of acres of swampy marshland, disease-infested dirty water, mosquitoes and 14,000 angry Indians who didn't want a bunch of strangers coming over and taking their land.

The settlers soon ran out of food; they'd been so busy looking for gold, they hadn't thought about farming. They'd all have died if it hadn't been for the help of a little girl. Pocahontas (which means 'Playful One') was ten years old when the settlers arrived. Her dad, the local Indian chief, didn't trust the newcomers, but Pocahontas was curious and liked a good laugh, and often visited the settlement to play with the young boys there.

When the settlers began to starve, she brought them food. Their leader, Captain John Smith, was taken captive by her father, but she pleaded for his life, and saved him from being executed. Eventually she married another of the English settlers and ended up going back home with him. Everybody in England wanted to meet a real-life Indian princess, and she was even introduced to the King!

Life back in Jamestown was getting worse – the settlers came close to giving up and going home. Some were reduced to eating bits of old boot and tree bark to stay alive. But with the help of fresh supplies of food and people, Jamestown eventually began to thrive.

By now other British settlements were springing up across the east coast of America and in nearby places, like Canada and the Caribbean. In spite of the hardship they faced, many British people were keen to leave home and set up in the New World. It offered a fresh start, freedom and an opportunity to make your fortune; and if you had to eat the odd boot along the way, well so what?

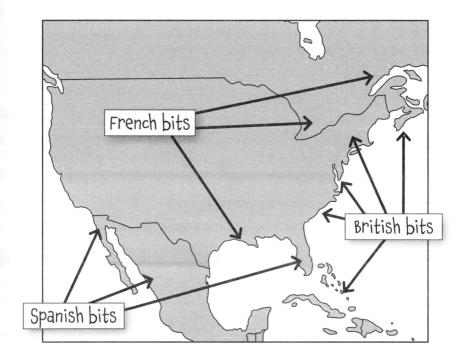

Settlers started big farms called plantations, growing crops like tobacco and cotton; but the crop that really caught the public's imagination was sugar!

SUGARED GHERKINS

In the seventeenth century most people in Britain had never tasted sugar, but very quickly they discovered how great it was. They started putting it in hot drinks, cold drinks, jams, jellies, ice cream, biscuits, pies and cakes. They dipped every food they could think of in sugar, and made scrummy little snacks out of it, like sugared fruit, sugared nuts, sugared flowers, sugared bark, sugared carrots and even sugared gherkins.

Everybody went sugar mad! The more they ate, the more sugar needed to be grown, and the more sugar the settlers grew, the more everyone ate. Sugar was big business!

There was just one snag. It doesn't grow in little packets on sugar trees. Making sugar is hard work . . . nightmarishly horrible hard work!!

Feel like a spoonful of sugar? OK . . .

Peewee's guide to . . .
MAKING SUGAR

1 Chop down a small forest, clear all the bushes and shrubs, and plant the area with sugar-cane seeds.

2 When the cane has grown big and thick, cut it and strip it. Mind you don't slash your hands on the sharp, spiky leaves or get big splinters under your fingernails.

3 Once you've cut several bundles of cane, tie them up, heave one on to your back, and carry it to the mill. Keep carrying the bundles until there's a huge pile of them on the mill floor.

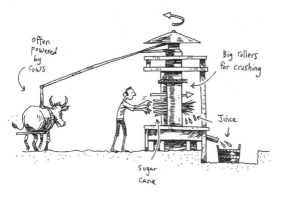

often powered by cows

Big rollers for crushing

Juice

Sugar cane

4 Now feed the bundles into the massive chopping, shredding and squeezing machines. Don't push your hands in too far, or your fingers will be chopped and shredded and squeezed too!

5 After several days, when you've squeezed all the juice out of the mushed-up cane, pour the liquid into a big vat and boil it up five or six times, standing over it with a ladle to scoop the scum off the top. You may fall in and get boiled alive, but even if you don't, you'll probably get a few nasty burns and pass out from the heat.

SUGAR

zzzzz

6 Allow the mixture to cool. When it's turned into crystals, get your spoon out, and shovel a great dollop of the stuff into your face. (Actually you'll probably be so exhausted you won't bother.)

THE CRUEL WORLD OF THE SLAVES

The plantation owners needed lots of workers to do this kind of work; ideally people who enjoyed doing horrible jobs day in and day out in hot and dangerous conditions for no money. Unfortunately, such people don't exist.

So they used people who didn't want to do it; people who they dragged from their own country in chains; people who were never allowed to return to their own homes ever again – in other words ... SLAVES.

Buying and selling slaves became an even bigger business than sugar! Slave traders in Africa kidnapped millions of men, women and children and sold them to British merchants, who transported them all the way across the Atlantic to America. The journey was a killer. The slavers crammed as many slaves as possible into their ships. They were chained together head-to-toe, in dark, dirty compartments below decks. It took two months to cross the ocean. Many slaves never made it, and their dead bodies were thrown over the side into the sea.

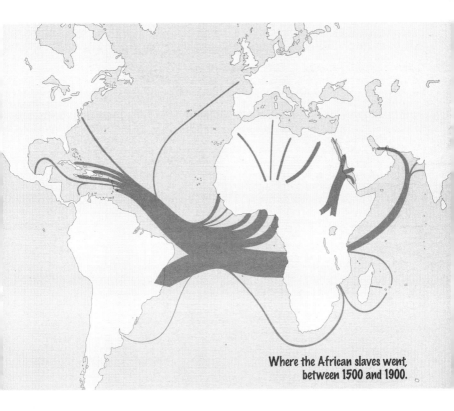

Where the African slaves went, between 1500 and 1900.

Those who survived were sold to the plantation owners in exchange for cotton, tobacco and sugar, which the slave-ships took back to Europe to sell for a big profit. Meanwhile the slaves were condemned to a lifetime of back-breaking work. They were beaten if they didn't do what they were told, and killed if they caused trouble.

British merchants got rich from selling slaves . . .

British plantation owners got rich from using slaves . . .

The British government got rich from taxing the merchants and the plantation owners . . .

The only people who lost out were . . .

35

GRACE'S TOP TEN BRITISH COLONIES

The British went all over the world nabbing bits of territory and turning them into 'colonies' – this meant they became part of the British Empire, even though they weren't in Britain or anywhere near it. Here's my guide to the 'top ten colonies' of the Empire . . .

10. THE POTATO-EATING COLONY

The British got a taste for creating colonies way back in medieval times, when the King of England, Henry II, looked across the Irish Sea to the country next door, and decided that he wanted to be King of Ireland too. English barons moved to Ireland and started building big castles and telling the Irish what to do. They called the area they lived in 'the Pale', and everything beyond it was 'beyond the Pale'. Over time, the English took over most of Ireland, and gave it to English, Welsh and Scottish farmers (in fact almost anyone who wasn't Irish), who first started growing the exotic new product of the New World . . . the potato! The Irish thought this was very unfair and spent the next 400 years trying to get their country back. Meanwhile, the English looked around to see who else they could colonize . . .

OK, we've got some chips . . .

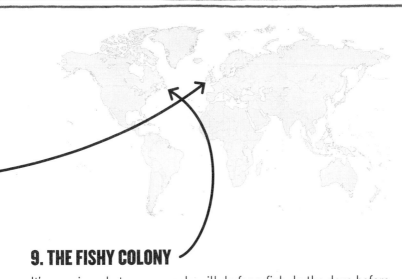

9. THE FISHY COLONY

It's amazing what some people will do for a fish. In the days before refrigerators, fish were a cheap and easy source of protein that didn't go bad if you stored them: you just covered them in salt, dried them out and kept them in the cupboard until you felt a bit peckish. The Vikings were the first Europeans to travel all the way to Canada in search of a nice bit of fish. Later on, in 1497, explorer John Cabot arrived at the island of Newfoundland. His sailors lowered buckets on ropes into the water and when they pulled them back up they were filled with fish. In fact his ship got stuck in the water because he was surrounded by so many cod! News got round, and Britain claimed Newfoundland as theirs – before anyone else could get their mitts on all that fishy goodness!

And a nice piece of fish!

Continued on page 61 . . .

FREE RUM INCLUDED

The English may have been a bit slow sailing across the world, finding new countries, sticking their flags in the sand, and claiming them for Britain, but once they'd got the hang of the idea, they started claiming countries like there was no tomorrow. (It didn't seem to matter if there were other people living there already: the Brits decided that if they weren't Europeans, they weren't important!)

Oi, you can't do that! This land is ours.

I think you'll find it's ours now.

Soon Britain had lots and lots of colonies, but it also had a big problem. How was it going to stop other countries from nicking them?

The best way was to have a top-notch navy: one that had lots of big, shiny, fast ships which could beat everyone else's navy, and could sail around the world making sure your colonies weren't about to be attacked. So, in the 1700s, the British put loads of money into building state-of-the-art ships, and tripled the size of their fleet.

Over the next century the Brits fought the Dutch, the Spanish and the French Navies – and beat them all! By 1815, the British Royal Navy had achieved its ambition, and had become the biggest and the best in the world . . . You couldn't sneeze in the middle of the ocean without the Royal Navy knowing about it and coming to see what you were up to. And in case anyone was in any doubt about who was in charge, they even made up a popular song about it.

Rule, Britannia, Britannia rules the waves. Britons never, never, never shall be slaves!*

* Unlike quite a lot of other people . . .

FLOATING CITIES

The largest ships in the Royal Navy were absolutely humungous – the biggest of them had three decks, 100 guns sticking out of the sides, and over 800 crew members! (Which is probably more than all the people in your entire school.)

Ships in those days didn't have an engine at the back to drive them along: instead they were powered by huge sails. The biggest ships had four and a half acres of sail; if you'd taken those sails down and put them side by side they'd have covered more than two football pitches!

This happens every time we play the Navy.

And to hoist all those sails up the masts, they had twenty-six miles of rope, some of it thicker than your arm. No wonder it took hundreds of people to sail a ship that size!

But as the boats got bigger and the number of them grew, the Navy needed more people; and when they ran out of sailors, they grabbed people off the street . . .

43

OI, YOU!

In the eighteenth century, the British Navy 'pressed' people into service; which means they forced you to join, even if you didn't want to.

'Press Gangs' would roam the streets looking for men aged between 18 and 45. When they found some likely-looking lads (usually in a pub) they'd set up a table and start asking for volunteers.

Roll up, roll up! Sign here and join the Navy. You look like a fun-loving adventurer, young sir. How would you like to earn your living seeing the world on one of His Majesty's finest ships? Spend all your time sunbathing and watching dolphins? Free rum included?

You must be joking!

If this method failed, they'd try to you make you sign up by getting you drunk.

Absolutely no way!

And if that didn't work, they'd bop you on the head and drag you unconscious onto the nearest ship, and you'd eventually wake up 1,000 miles out to sea with a splitting headache and two years to wait before you got back home.

You didn't even have to be able to swim! In fact, not being able to swim was considered an advantage. If you fell overboard, nobody was going to turn one of those great big ships around to come and pick you back up, so the quicker you drowned the better!

THE RELUCTANT SAILOR

Absolutely way!

SKYLARKS AND POWDER MONKEYS

It wasn't just men who joined the Royal Navy – kids did as well! Boys as young as ten ran away to sea (it must have seemed a better life than staying at home bored to death, and earning no money).

The small, nimble ones were employed running up and down the rigging, which was a network of ropes hanging 200 feet above the ocean waves. Some boys got so good at it they did it for fun; this was known as 'skylarking'.

Some were employed as cabin boys. They ran messages from one end of the ship to the other, helped the cook out in the ship's galley (the kitchen), and carried food to the tables at mealtimes.

Come on, it's easy!

I think I'll stay down here and become an officer.

Others became 'powder monkeys', who ran bags of gunpowder to the guns in the heat of battle.

Note: Do not try this at home. Running gunpowder is a highly dangerous activity. If you fall over you are likely to explode, leaving a large smoking hole in the floor, and bits of you splattered all over the wallpaper. So don't do it.

Life on board was tough, and a lot of kids were killed. But if you survived for long enough, you might even become an officer one day!

THE 18TH-CENTURY ASTRONAUT

That's exactly what happened to James Cook. He first went to sea when he was seventeen. He wanted to go where no man had gone before, and explore the furthest corners of the oceans. If he'd been alive today, he'd probably have become an astronaut.

He was a brilliant navigator, and in the 1770s he led a Royal Naval expedition to explore the Pacific Ocean. While he was there he found an enormous land full of kangaroos and koalas, stuck a Union Jack in the sand, and claimed Australia as a brand-new part of the British Empire.

TATTOOS AND SEVERED HEADS

Cook's crew were some of the first Europeans to get tattoos! They'd seen them on New Zealand's Maori (pronounced 'Mow-ree') tribesmen. Tattoos became all the rage among sailors and even Queen Victoria's son Edward got one!

If you didn't want your own tatt, you could try and get hold of the tattooed head of a Maori tribesman to put in your home! It had been a traditional custom for the Maori to preserve the heads of their dead chiefs, and Cook's crew brought four back to England. They proved so popular that a brisk trade in heads sprang up, until it was eventually banned in 1831!

Everyone thought Cook was a great hero, and the Navy eventually made him a Captain – not bad for someone who'd started his career as an ordinary seaman.

AN APPLE A DAY . . .

Explosions, tattoos, severed heads and fights with the natives – life on board a Royal Navy ship was dangerous, but at least it wasn't dull. What's more, you got regular hot meals (which you didn't always get on land). All that was missing was fresh fruit and veg. Food like apples, oranges, sprouts and spinach went rotten very quickly. After a few weeks at sea, the only green stuff left to eat was the mould growing on the meat.

I know what you're thinking: 'Life without Brussels sprouts sounds great!' But with no fruit and vegetables, sailors came down with a disgusting condition known as 'scurvy'. Their breath stank, their gums bled and their teeth fell out, their skin turned black, they became so weak they couldn't stand up, and then they died.

All sorts of experiments were made, but eventually it was realized that if you drank a cup of lemon juice it cleared up scurvy in a matter of days.

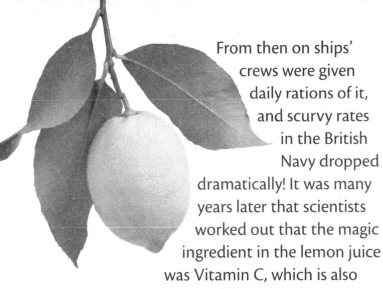

From then on ships' crews were given daily rations of it, and scurvy rates in the British Navy dropped dramatically! It was many years later that scientists worked out that the magic ingredient in the lemon juice was Vitamin C, which is also found in fresh fruit and vegetables.

So now you know about scurvy, maybe you'll eat up your greens (OK, probably not the sprouts).

I could murder a lemon!

Please don't!

A GOOD DRINK AND A GOOD FIGHT

Food wasn't the only thing that went off on board ship. There was no drinking water because it went manky so quickly. Instead sailors washed their food down with eight pints of beer and a daily rum ration. Even the boys got a tot of rum!

When sailors get drunk, they often kick off a bit, but those who caused trouble in the British Navy were flogged with the dreaded cat-o'-nine-tails – a whip made of nine strands of rope, each with a big fat knot at the end. A few strokes with the 'cat' and your back turned to jelly . . . Aarrrrgghh!

Serious crimes like mutinies (which tended to occur when you tried to cancel the crew's rum ration) were supposed to be punished by hanging. But this didn't often happen. Sailors were so valuable to the Navy, that officers thought it was a terrible waste to hang them, even the ones who were mutinous drunkards!

Napoleon

THE SEASICK HERO

In 1805, the British Navy was put to its biggest test.

France and Spain had joined forces under the leadership of the French ruler and military genius Napoleon Bonaparte, or 'Boney' as the English called him. He didn't just want to get his hands on Britain's colonies, he wanted to conquer Britain! But he knew that in order to do that, he'd first have to defeat the British Navy. So he assembled a massive invasion fleet.

Nelson

Standing in Boney's way was Admiral Horatio Nelson. Nelson had gone to sea when he was twelve, and despite suffering from terrible seasickness, malaria and a bout of scurvy, as well as losing an eye and one of his arms in battle, he had risen through the ranks to become Britain's best naval commander (when he wasn't throwing up over the side of his ship).

On 20 October 1805, Boney's fleet left the port of Cadiz in Spain, but the British were lying in wait. Nelson ordered his men to prepare for battle . . .

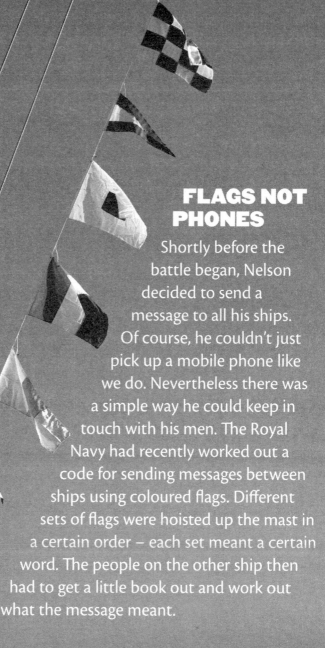

FLAGS NOT PHONES

Shortly before the battle began, Nelson decided to send a message to all his ships. Of course, he couldn't just pick up a mobile phone like we do. Nevertheless there was a simple way he could keep in touch with his men. The Royal Navy had recently worked out a code for sending messages between ships using coloured flags. Different sets of flags were hoisted up the mast in a certain order – each set meant a certain word. The people on the other ship then had to get a little book out and work out what the message meant.

Nelson was sensible and kept his message short!
'England expects that every man will do his duty', was
all it said. In other words it didn't matter if you were a
captain or a cabin boy, a gunnery officer or a powder
monkey; everyone was in this fight together. Sailors at
that time were used to being treated as the lowest of
the low. To be told they were as good as their officers
inspired them to do their best.

The British finally met Boney's fleet off the coast of
Spain near a place called Trafalgar. Sea battles at that
time were mostly just a matter of firing off as many
shots as possible until the ship you were attacking sank
or surrendered.

DEATH BY SPLINTERS

If you were in a battle at sea and you were really unlucky, you might be hit by a cannonball. But you'd be more likely to be killed by a splinter. I don't mean a tiny little thing the size of an ant's leg that sticks in your thumb and makes you whinge a bit – I'm talking about chunks of wood as big as a man's arm and as sharp as a razor. These were caused by cannonballs blasting massive holes in the sides of the wooden ship, which came hurtling through the air towards you at 100 miles per hour.

The packed gun-decks quickly filled with smoke from the cannons, and the floors became slippery with blood and guts from the dead and dying.

If you were hit, your only hope was that it was in a part of your body that you didn't need, like an arm or the leg. Then you'd be carried to the surgeon's table and your injured limb would be sawn off and thrown in a bucket. The stump was then sewn up and you lay down and hoped you'd get better.

With no anaesthetic to dull the pain and no antiseptic to kill the bacteria, your chances of survival were pretty slim.

Nelson's Navy fought bravely and managed to defeat Boney's men. Unfortunately, Admiral Nelson didn't survive. He was shot on the deck of his ship HMS *Victory*, and died below decks just hours after learning that he'd won the battle.

Sailors who died at sea were usually sewn into their hammocks, with cannon shot to weigh them down and the last stitch passed through their nose (to make sure they were really dead), before being dropped into the sea. But this didn't happen to Nelson – his body was put in a barrel of brandy to preserve it, then it was taken back to Britain, where he was given a hero's funeral in London. His victory had saved Britain from invasion and proved that Britain really did rule the waves!

I hate pigeons even more than I hate the French.

I'm your worst nightmare – a French pigeon!

THE ANTI-SLAVERY SQUADRON

Ruling the waves meant that the Royal Navy had to be a sort of floating police force – it kept an eye on everything that was going on and put a stop to anything it didn't like.

In 1807, the British government finally made it illegal to sell or buy slaves. Any British ship found carrying them was fined £100 for each slave on board, and any foreign ship containing slaves was confiscated.

A Royal Navy squadron was sent to patrol the coast around Africa. Over the next fifty years it seized or destroyed more than 1,500 slave ships and released more than 150,000 Africans.

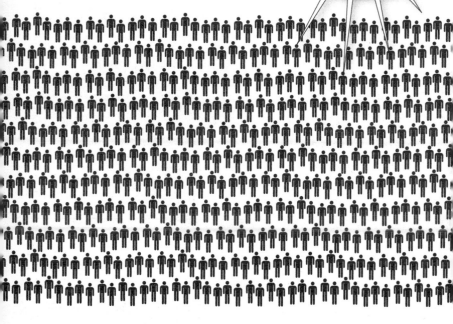

About time, too!

GRACE'S TOP TEN BRITISH COLONIES

8. THE MYSTERY COLONY

The first attempts by the British to set up a colony in North America ended pretty badly for the colonists. In 1585 a group of 100 English colonists set up home on the island of Roanoke. But before long they got into a fight with the local Indians, who refused to give them any food and left them to starve to death, so they gave up and went home. Two years later in 1587 a second group of colonists pitched up and tried to make a go of it. After several months, their leader returned home to England to ask for help, and when he finally got back, all the buildings had been dismantled and everyone had disappeared – to this day nobody knows what happened to them . . . Weird or what?

Maybe they just popped out to the shops and got lost.

GRACE'S TOP TEN BRITISH COLONIES

7. THE SMOKERS' COLONY

Some colonies were set up by businessmen trying to strike it rich. They took over land to grow things like:

sugar ...

Which you put in sweets.

cocoa ...

Which you put in chocolate.

rubber ...

Which you put in, erm ... rubber balls.

and tobacco ...

Which is stinky and makes you cough!

TOBACCO LEAVES

Tobacco leaves you with a bad cough!

The American Indians had been smoking tobacco for centuries, but the Europeans had only just found out about it and pretty soon they were completely hooked! In 1607, a group of businessmen sent settlers off to found a colony called Virginia in North America. They grew tobacco plants, shipped the leaves back to Europe and made a fortune – helping to make the British Empire rich!

Continued on page 84 . . .

POWERING AN EMPIRE

By 1800 Britain had a nice little Empire, including bits of Canada, Africa, India and Australia, and it had a killer navy to protect them.

But running an Empire that stretched across millions of miles and several oceans was a pain in the bum. It took ages to get from one part of the Empire to another (for instance the journey to Canada took about six weeks, and getting to India took up to four months!), which meant that travellers were always late, messages were

Sorry, I can't hear you.

out of date when they arrived, and basically nobody had a clue what was going on!

Fortunately, in the nineteenth century British engineers and scientists invented lots of handy new machines that made running an enormous Empire a lot easier. Whizz-bang new technology like steam trains, steam ships and the telegraph linked all the different parts of the Empire together, making it easier to travel around, send messages and generally know what was going on in faraway places. The Brits used this new technology to make their Empire bigger and more efficient!

THE STEAM HORSE

Perhaps the greatest invention ever to come out of Great Britain was the steam engine.

OK . . . so it doesn't sound like the most exciting thing ever invented. An engine that makes steam? I get buckets of steam every time I run a bath and nobody ever called me a genius.

But the steam produced by steam engines could be used to power all sorts of machines, making them work faster and harder than ever before. Steam engines were put into factories, mills and mines all around Britain so that they could produce more and more stuff like iron, steel and coal.

Soon Britain had iron, steel and coal coming out of its ears – so it shipped it all around the world and sold it for huge amounts of money. The steam engine made Britain rich.

And then some clever-clogs decided to put one on wheels . . .

HOW TO INVENT A STEAM ENGINE

The brainbox who did this was a Cornishman called Richard Trevithick. When he was a boy no one would have guessed that one day he'd do something brilliant. His teachers thought he wasn't very bright – one called him disobedient, slow, obstinate and inattentive! But much to everyone's surprise, he grew up to be an engineering whizz (so if you've ever had a bad school report, rest easy – you're probably a genius in waiting).

Richard's dad had run a mine and whenever he'd had some free time, young Richard had tinkered with the engines, making them work better and seeing what new things he could make them do.

You can just imagine it, can't you – there he was, hanging around the mine, nothing to do, watching a steam engine chugging away . . .

Hmm! I wonder what'll happen if I fix this engine upside down on the roof.

No – not a good idea.

And ta-da! The steam train was born (or the 'steam horse' as it was originally known).

HORSE

STEAM HORSE

Trevithick showed people his first working railway steam locomotive in 1804. It was designed to carry iron and coal from the mines and it was incredibly slow, taking four hours to travel just nine miles!

SPEED KILLS!

Twenty-five years later another engineer, George Stephenson, designed a train that became known as 'The Rocket'. He built it for a competition to invent a fast steam train that could carry people from Liverpool to Manchester. Races were held over several days to see whose train was best, and 15,000 people saw Stephenson's 'Rocket' become the clear winner, reaching speeds up to 29 mph!

That may not sound very fast either, but in an age when everybody either walked everywhere or rode a horse, people weren't used to travelling at speed. Some scientists said that your brain would stop working if you travelled at 20 mph, and anyone going at more than 30 mph would have all the air sucked out of them and would suffocate to death. (I don't think this is true, but it might be worth checking next time you're in a car.)

Trains may not have melted people's brains or sucked the air out of their lungs, but they were still potential killers.

On the opening day of the Liverpool-to-Manchester railway in 1830, one of the spectators, William Huskisson, stood on the railway track to get a closer look, couldn't get out of the way in time, and was knocked over by 'The Rocket' on its way to Manchester! On being hit he is supposed to have said, 'I have met my death.' He was spot on. He died that evening.

In 1842 Queen Victoria became the first British monarch to ride a train – the Great Western Railway built a special royal carriage to take her from Slough to London Paddington. She was so 'charmed' by the experience that she regularly started going on trains – although she didn't like it if they started going fast, and insisted that they stopped whenever she wanted to eat or go to the loo!

Stop the train, One needs a wee.

By 1845 over two thousand miles of railway criss-crossed Britain, and 30 million passengers were travelling by train each year!

GOOD QUEEN VIC

For 63 years, the entire British Empire was ruled by one woman . . . Queen Victoria. She was the longest reigning Queen in world history!

In pictures she often looks like a dumpy little sour-faced old woman dressed in black. But she wasn't always that way!

When she became Queen of Great Britain in 1837, she was just eighteen! A typical teenager, she enjoyed having a laugh, riding horses really fast, going to parties and flirting with boys!

A couple of years later, she fell madly in love with her cousin Albert. She wrote in her diary about how good-looking he was with his delicate moustache and exquisite nose! They married soon afterwards and together they had nine children and forty grandchildren! It was after he died that she got really sad, and started looking grumpy.

Who's that grumpy . . . Oh, it's me in fifty years' time!

Victoria lived until 1901 and under her the British Empire grew into the biggest Empire in history! It's because of her that we call this time the 'Victorian Period' and the people who lived in her lifetime the 'Victorians'.

But it didn't stop there. The Brits built railways all over their Empire: through India, up Africa and across Canada, knitting the different parts of the Empire together. Trains made getting round the British Empire a doddle; instead of taking months hiking across hills, hacking through forest and wading through rivers, you could now simply buy a train ticket! So more and more people left Britain and travelled abroad to set up home in faraway places like Africa or India.

But trains didn't just carry people. They were used to transport animals, food, letters, newspapers, cotton, iron, steel, anything you can think of, to shops and factories all over the Empire. And as more of these things were sold, so the Empire got richer and richer!

Trains helped sort out trouble too. If there was a bit of aggravation anywhere in the Empire, the British sent trains full of soldiers to stamp it out.

FIRE!

It wasn't just trains that made travel easier. Britain began building massive steam-powered ships!

The SS ('Steam Ship') *Great Western* made its first voyage across the Atlantic in 1838. The trip wasn't a spectacular success – on its way from London to Bristol a fire broke out in the engine room, and all but seven passengers cancelled their trip! Still, it made it to New York and it wasn't long before 'steamers' were crossing weekly to America and back. Crossing the ocean now took weeks rather than months!

I said hurry up!!!

The *Great Western* had paddle wheels on the sides, rather than a propeller at the back. And sails for when the engines broke down!

AN ELECTRIFYING NEW DISCOVERY!

From the 1750s onwards scientists all over the world were experimenting with electricity. They did lots of crazy experiments like flying kites in storms to try and capture the lightning flashing across the sky.

Of course, you and I know that this is really dumb behaviour, because electricity is dangerous and you could end up with sticky-out hair and fried eyeballs. But these nutty scientists found this out the hard way . . .

In 1753, a German called Georg Wilhelm Richmann tried to capture the electricity in a storm cloud by using a long metal rod attached to the roof of his house. He was struck by lightning which killed him stone dead and blew both his shoes off!

Fortunately for scientists everywhere, they finally worked out better ways to generate electricity using things like chemical reactions and magnets. It wasn't long before electricity was being used to power a whole new generation of machines!

'T-MAIL'

Even with the invention of steam trains and steam ships, sending messages from one place to another still took quite a long time. You couldn't just send someone an e-mail or a text, you had to sit down and write a letter using a pen and paper. It took ages and the ink got everywhere! Then you had to take your letter to the post office and wait weeks or even months for it to arrive at the other end.

But once people knew how to use electricity, they were able to come up with a new invention that solved the problem of slow messages – the telegraph. Electrical signals sent a special code of long and short pulses down wires that were laid along the side of railway tracks. Messages could now be sent and received in the blink of an eye!

Mind you, it took a while for people to realize how useful this new invention was. For ten years the only people who sent telegrams were train operators, who used them to tell railway station masters what time the next train was coming in. But in 1844 two pick-pockets escaped from London on a train bound for Slough. The police telegraphed

Slough Station to tell them the criminals were coming, and as soon as they got out of the train, they were arrested.

Suddenly everyone wanted to send telegrams!

In 1866 a telegraph cable was laid under the Atlantic Ocean stretching all the way from Britain to America; in 1870 another was laid from Britain to India; and in 1872 one was laid all the way to Australia . . . The British Empire was going online (well, sort of!).

THE GREAT EXHIBITION OF GREAT THINGS FROM GREAT BRITAIN

The British were really proud of all their inventions; they thought that Britain had the best scientists, the best engineers and the best inventors in the world! So, to show off everything that was great about Britain and its Empire, they decided to hold a great exhibition.

It was called (surprise, surprise) 'The Great Exhibition' and it was held inside a ginormous glass building called the 'Crystal Palace', which had been designed especially for it (imagine a greenhouse the size of a multi-storey car park).

Queen Victoria described the opening of the Exhibition as the happiest day of her life. She loved it so much that she visited it 33 times over the five months it was on! But the Queen wasn't the only visitor; over six million people came to see it!

They saw demonstrations of machines like steam engines and the telegraph, along with all sorts of other things like an early type of fax machine, a sewing machine, printing machines, drilling machines and a machine for putting corks in bottles.

But not all the inventions were so useful. Some inventors got carried away and came up with some pretty weird stuff . . .

DR GEORGE MERRYWEATHER'S 'TEMPEST PROGNOSTICATOR'

Leeches are tiny slug-like creatures that suck blood from animals and humans. The aptly named Dr Merryweather believed they could be used to predict changes in weather. He designed a machine made up of 12 glass bottles each containing a leech, which were connected to a small bell using various wires, chains and bits of whalebone. When the leeches sensed a change in the atmosphere they were supposed to climb up their bottles and trigger the bell.

THE ALARM CLOCK BED

The inventor Theophilius Carter came up with an ingenious 'silent alarm clock bed' – a clockwork bed that tipped its occupant out on to the floor at the appointed time!

THE TOO-BIG-FOR-YOUR-POCKET PENKNIFE

The Victorians LOVED penknives. For the Great Exhibition, a Sheffield cutler made a gigantic two-and-half-foot-long pocket-knife with 75 blades, saws, hooks, picks and assorted gadgetry, all engraved with pictures of famous buildings and people.

LIEUTENANT HALKETT'S INDIA RUBBER BOAT-CLOAK

Rubber was a newly discovered material that enabled the Victorians to come up with lots of useful inventions like bicycle tyres, mackintoshes, rubber bands and wellington boots, as well as some not-so-useful ones . . . like an inflatable boat-cloak – a rubber cloak that could be pumped up with bellows stored in one pocket, and steered with paddles stored in the other!

THE PUBLIC TOILET

Some of the first public toilets (or 'monkey closets' as they were known) were installed at the Great Exhibition. More than 800,000 people paid a penny to use them – which is where the term 'spend a penny' comes from! Unfortunately, once you were inside you had to keep one hand firmly on the door handle, because they didn't have locks. The vacant/engaged bolt wasn't invented until 30 years later!

Alongside all the crazy new gadgets and gizmos at the Exhibition,were objects from countries all around the British Empire: a fire-engine from Canada, an ivory-carved throne from India, tropical flowers and fruits from the West Indies, gold from Australia and metalwork from Africa. These displays showed just how huge the British Empire was and all the amazing places and people that were part of it!

GRACE'S TOP TEN BRITISH COLONIES

6. THE PIRATE COLONY

Jamaica is a large island in the Caribbean, which was a useful stop-off on the way to and from America. So the British grabbed it from the Spanish in 1655. But you would have been mad to stop there long because, although it was supposed to be a British colony, it was run by pirates – yes, real pirates with names like Blackbeard and Calico Jack! They defended the island from attack in return for being allowed to operate out of the capital city, Port Royal, although they spent most of their time gambling, drinking rum and singing sea-shanties with bar-maids. There were so many pubs in Port Royal that even the island's parrots were said to get drunk every night! It was known as the 'richest and wickedest city in the world'! Maybe I'll book my next holiday there . . .

5. THE TATTOOED COLONY

When the British first arrived in New Zealand in 1769 it was inhabited by scary-looking tribes called the Maori, who were tall, strong, had strange spiral tattoos all over their faces and bodies and did scary war-dances. Fights broke out, the British pushed the Maori off their land and the Maori fought back. The British eventually won and New Zealand became a British colony.

Continued on page 105 . . .

THE JEWEL IN THE CROWN

Among the thousands of amazing exhibits on display at the Great Exhibition was a diamond. But it wasn't just any old diamond . . . it was the largest diamond in the world – the size of a hen's egg!

I wouldn't fancy laying that!

It was called the 'Kohinoor Diamond' (pronounced 'Coe-i-noor'), which means 'Mountain of Light', and it had come all the way from India!

Unfortunately, thousands of the people who queued up to see it thought it was rubbish – they complained that it wasn't sparkly enough! You just can't please some folk, can you?

But there was another jewel that everyone was impressed by – India itself! It was known as 'The Jewel in the Crown of the British Empire' because it was so valuable: a country full of spices, cotton and tea, all of which could be shipped home by the boatload and sold in Europe for a massive profit.

BLACK GOLD

I expect you imagine that spices are nothing more than rather powerful-tasting powders in little jars in the kitchen spice-rack. But for centuries, they'd been almost as valuable as gold, and it was spices that first led British merchants to India.

I know what you're thinking: 'What's the big deal about spices? I'd rather have gold, diamonds or a new pair of trainers any day of the week.'

But imagine you were a British person sitting down to dinner 250 years ago and in front of you was a piece of meat. Most days you'd only get porridge and a few bits of veg, so this would be a really special occasion. Meat was a treat!

But because there weren't any refrigerators back then, the meat would have been sitting for weeks in a barrel of salt to try and stop it from going green, so it would have smelled funny, and tasted dry, hard and really salty.

Putting something spicy in your dinner to cover up the taste might suddenly seem like a really great idea – the stronger the better!

Pepper, cinnamon, cloves, ginger, bring them on!

Without them, mealtimes would be miserable, but mix them into your grub, and even the most rancid meat would taste like Christmas Day round Jamie Oliver's place.

The trouble was, though, that none of these spices grew in Europe. Pepper comes from India, cinnamon and ginger are from South East Asia, and cloves are from Indonesia. And because merchants had to travel such long distances to get hold of these gorgeous-smelling spices, and risked robbery or shipwreck along the way, they charged a fortune for them. In fact peppercorns were so valuable that they became known as 'Black Gold'!

A NICE HOT CUP OF ROSIE LEE

But it wasn't just spices that made the merchants big money. Here's a quiz . . .

Builders drink it in chipped mugs with three sugars . . .

Little old ladies sip it in dainty little cups with tiny cucumber sandwiches . . .

Fishermen slurp it out of flasks, and businessmen gulp it out of paper cups on their way to work . . .

What is it?

Nowadays we're all obsessed with tea! But it wasn't always like that. Back in the Middle Ages, Britain's favourite drink was beer!

Then British merchants set up a business called 'The East India Company' to control all the trade from the East, and started shipping over vast quantities of tea from China and India and selling it for a tidy profit to the posh people of Britain. The East India Company were the only people allowed to import tea, so they could charge whatever they liked. This made it dead expensive!

SHEEP-DUNG TEA

Dodgy street-traders made their own tea to sell to people who hadn't got much money. They collected used tea leaves from the servants of the rich, dried them out and mixed them with all sorts of disgusting things like iron filings, clay, plaster, sawdust, leaves from trees and even dried sheep dung! Then when they'd got a great big pile of the stuff, they put it into bags, and sold it cheap to anyone who fancied a nice cup of cut-price tea.

The East India Company was soon richer than a billionaire who's just won a rollover lottery prize. Eventually it became so big it was running most of India! Men who worked for it were governing towns and cities, collecting taxes and making laws. It was the most powerful company in the world, and even had its own army. This wasn't great news for the Indians; they were being ruled by greedy businessmen who were only interested in making more and more money!

THE MAN WHO SLEPT THROUGH A MUTINY!

By 1857 lots of Indians were fed up with being ruled by the East India Company, so they rebelled! Thousands of them, from ordinary farmers to wealthy Indian princes, rose up against British rule, and they were even joined by some of the Indian soldiers in the Company's army.

In the city of Lucknow, the rebels attacked the big house belonging to the British governor. Inside were 2,000 Britons, including women and children. They were trapped in the house for five months. Eventually they sneaked out hidden by canvas screens while British troops fired on the attacking Indians. They all managed to escape . . . Well, all except one. A young soldier called Captain Thomas Waterman was fast asleep in bed and only woke up two hours after the others had got out. Imagine how scared he must have been when he opened his eyes and found that the place was deserted!

With 30,000 angry Indians surrounding the house, Thomas couldn't stroll out of the gate.

How come he'd been left all on his own?

Maybe he was dead unpopular and the others decided to leave without him!

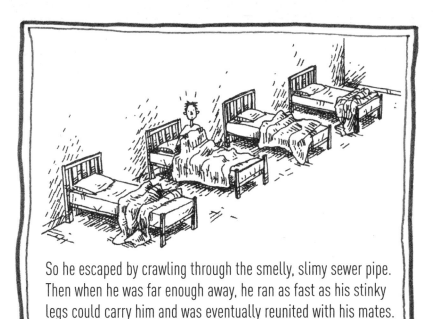

So he escaped by crawling through the smelly, slimy sewer pipe. Then when he was far enough away, he ran as fast as his stinky legs could carry him and was eventually reunited with his mates.

British troops were sent from all over the Empire to help stamp out the rebellion. They didn't take any prisoners. Anyone suspected of being a rebel was bayoneted on the spot, or sentenced to some sort of gruesome public execution.

What kind of gruesome execution?

Trust me, you don't want to know. But it involves me . . .

A NOT-SO-BRIGHT IDEA

British soldiers were originally known as 'red-coats' because of their bright red uniforms. Wearing a smart red coat might have made you look super-cool, but the enemy could see you coming a mile off – a bit like having a big flashing sign on your head saying 'Please fire at this spot!'

So during the Indian Mutiny, a lot of British soldiers got rid of their red uniforms and started wearing sandy-brown clothes instead, and to make sure their white shirts didn't stand out, they dyed them by boiling them in tea.

The new colour they'd invented became known as 'khaki' (which means 'dust' in Persian), and it rapidly became the standard colour of all army service uniforms!

After the rebellion, it was decided that it wasn't such a good idea for India to be run by a load of bent businessmen. So from then on, Queen Victoria took charge, and she was called the 'Empress of India' (although she never actually set foot in India, because it was too far away!).

Instead she got a whole load of government officials and army officers to run it for her. They were known as 'The British Raj', 'Raj' being an Indian word for 'rule'. It was a big job – a few thousand British officials and troops ruling 300 million Indians!

MAGNIFICENT MOUSTACHES

If you've ever seen photos of men in the British Raj you might have noticed they're often shown wearing ridiculous moustaches which were known as mutton-chops, handle-bars, nose-bugs, crumb-catchers, lady-ticklers and soup-strainers!

When the Brits had first arrived in India, most of them had smooth top lips. But the Indians, who thought a big moustache made you look a real man, nearly wet themselves laughing!

This didn't go down very well with the British, who didn't like being laughed at by a bunch of locals. So they started growing moustaches too, and as time went on, their face-hair grew bigger and more complicated!

The ends were curled, twirled or styled with wax until they stuck out like daggers. Dozens of little brushes and combs were designed to get the most out of them. There was even a special 'moustache spoon' with a lip on it to stop the gentleman's moustache from getting wet when he ate soup!

By the end of the nineteenth century, the British took their facial hair so seriously that an explorer called Richard Burton even challenged a man to a duel for laughing at his moustache!

'RUFFIAN DICK' BURTON

The furthest corners of the British Empire attracted plenty of oddball explorers in search of adventure. Perhaps none so odd or tough as Richard 'Ruffian Dick' Burton. Six foot in his socks, Burton was a fierce and fiery-tempered soldier who said he had joined the East India Company's army because, he was 'fit for nothing but to be shot at for sixpence a day'.

But he had a successful and adventure-packed life as a soldier, spy, explorer, writer (one of his books is a history of farting), translator, poet and amateur hypnotist! He had a real talent for languages and ended up being able to speak more than twenty-five of them. He even kept a pack of tame monkeys in the hope that he might be able to learn how they spoke!

Once he was attacked by Somali warriors and a javelin went straight through his mouth. Incredibly, he remained conscious and managed to make his escape with the weapon still sticking out of him!

Let me out!

Burton translated *The Arabian Nights* into English, including the story of Aladdin and his magic lamp.

ALL THE RAGE IN THE RAJ

If you and your family had moved to India from Britain, life there would be pretty cushy. You'd have lived in a big house with lots of servants who did everything for you – some of the top officials had up to 400 of them! Compared to the native Indians, you'd have been a millionaire!

Not that you got to know your servants. You were expected to spend your time with the other British families attending tea parties and picnics, playing tennis, cricket and croquet. For the more adventurous there were horse races, gambling or going off to shoot tigers!

But it wasn't all fun and games in the British Raj. If you were unlucky enough to be posted to some remote faraway place, life got pretty dull. Travel was so difficult you couldn't go anywhere much, and there were lots of disgusting killer diseases around.

Europeans wore lightweight helmets to keep the sun off their delicate white heads. They were made of pith (the middle of reeds), covered in cloth and had holes for ventilation.

HUNTING TIGERS!

British officials loved killing big animals. Their idea of a good time was polishing their rifles, climbing on top of an elephant and trotting off into the jungle to bag themselves a tiger . . . the bigger and more ferocious the better!

Spectacular hunts were arranged each year, and their wives were invited to come and watch them blasting away! All this was fine unless you were the tiger, or one of the unlucky Indians chosen to be the 'beaters', who were sent out on foot to whack the long grass with sticks, or bang drums and crash cymbals to wake up the tigers and drive them towards the elephants!

This kind of hunting became so popular that India began to run out of tigers. One army officer, Colonel William Rice, shot 158 in just four years!

The weather got so unbearably hot in summer that whole households moved up into the hills where it was cooler. Teams of camels carried pots and pans, clothes, iron baths and even pianos for miles, so the sweaty British families could set up second homes for a few months.

And being a kid in British India was particularly dull. You'd be looked after by your servants until you reached the age of seven, then you'd be packed off to boarding school back in England to get a 'proper' education. It might be ten years before you saw your family again!

British children with their Indian servants in 1910.

CURRY-TASTIC!

The British who lived in India came back home with quite a few native words we still use today. If you ever find yourself in a **bungalow**, and decide to take off your **dungarees** and put on your **pyjamas**, you'll be using three words that come from India. (Although whose bungalow it'll be, and why you'll be going to bed in it, I have no idea!)

But far and away the most popular thing to come from India was the food! The British in India were said to eat curry for breakfast, lunch and dinner, and they brought their taste for it back home with them! It wasn't just curry they liked, though. There was rice pudding, brown sauce, chutney, pickles, kedgeree and a weird-sounding, peppery broth called mulligatawny soup.

The first Indian restaurant in London, 'the Hindoostanee Coffee House', was opened in 1809. Even Queen Victoria was a fan of curry. She employed her very own Indian servant who cooked the Queen's curries just the way she liked them!

GRACE'S TOP TEN BRITISH COLONIES

4. THE MONKEY COLONY

When the British captured Gibraltar from the Spanish in 1704, it had no farmland and no fresh water, and the only residents were a bunch of monkeys (who were probably a bit miffed when they realized that the British hadn't brought any bananas with them). But even though Gibraltar was just a big barren Spanish rock sticking out into the sea, it was in a really useful place, smack bang at the entrance to the Mediterranean Sea. From it Britain could keep an eye on the thousands of ships that passed by every year. They turned it into a heavily fortified military and naval base. It was used all the way up to World War Two, when miles of tunnels and caverns were dug into it to form an 'underground city' complete with barracks, offices, frozen meat store, bakery and a fully equipped hospital! Even today the British flag flies over Gibraltar, which makes the Spanish very cross.

GRACE'S TOP TEN BRITISH COLONIES

3. THE STROPPY COLONIES

In 1776 all the colonists in America got together and wrote to King George III telling him that they didn't want to be part of the British Empire any more; instead they were going to do their own thing. They said that everyone should be equal (in other words no more kings) and that all citizens had the right to freedom and happiness. This was pretty revolutionary stuff . . .

No more kings? What do we do with all the gold pointy hats? If we give people freedom, does that mean we can't tell them what to do all the time? Happiness – what's that?

The British sent an army to America to try and keep control, but The Americans beat the Brits.

From now on we're going to call ourselves the 'United States of America'!

George Washington, the colonist who commanded the American forces, beat the Brits and became the first President.

Aren't we just the greatest? You betcha!

Continued on page 124 . . .

ADVENTURES IN AFRICA

Imagine an entire continent that's hot, sweaty and full of dense jungle and nasty creepy-crawlies. That's what a lot of Europeans believed Africa was like. They thought you'd have to be stark raving mad to go there, and even called it 'The Dark Continent'.

But in the 1850s attitudes began to change, and this was all down to one slightly mad Scotsman. David Livingstone was a man on a mission! He was a hard-working doctor, was seriously religious and desperately wanted to spread the wonders of civilization and Christianity to the darkest corners of the earth! You couldn't get much darker than the 'Dark Continent' itself, so in 1840 he jumped on a boat to Africa.

When he got there he realized that spreading civilization would be a whole lot easier if he actually knew what Africa looked like. Lots of Europeans had explored round its edges, but none of them had the faintest idea what was in the middle. So he decided to try and map the entire African interior.

Doesn't ANYONE here know how to tie a bow tie?

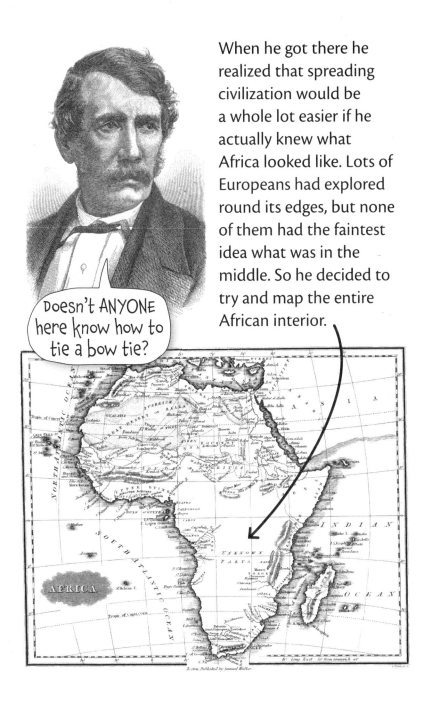

Eventually he became the first European to cross the continent from west to east. On one trip he came across a massive waterfall a mile wide and 350 feet high, which the locals called the 'Smoke that Thunders'. That seems a pretty good name for it, doesn't it? But he promptly renamed it 'Victoria Falls' in honour of British Queen Victoria. Not surprisingly, he was soon a national hero back in Britain.

Towards the end of his life, Livingstone became obsessed with one mission – to find the source of the Nile, the longest river in Africa. Many explorers before him had tried and failed, but Livingstone was convinced he was the man to do it!

The search drove him to distraction – he spent six years wandering all over the place trying to find where this massive river started (in fact lots of different rivers and lakes feed into the Nile, so it's difficult to know exactly where it begins, although it's probably somewhere in modern-day Rwanda).

Meanwhile Livingstone's porters deserted him, his emergency supplies were stolen, and he caught pneumonia, malaria, cholera, dysentery, and horrible foot ulcers! Eventually he lost contact with the outside world and word spread that he'd

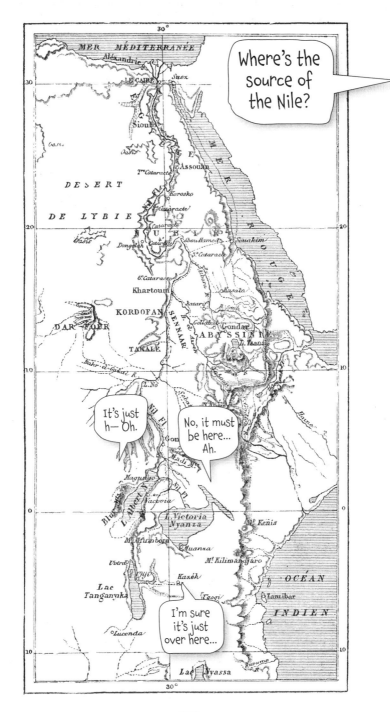

died. That would have been the end of him if it hadn't have been for the editors of an American newspaper called the *New York Herald*. They decided it would be the scoop of the decade if they could track the great explorer down. So they sent Henry Morton Stanley, their keenest young reporter, to see if Livingstone was still alive somewhere in the heart of the African jungle!

After eight months and a hellish 7,000-mile journey, Stanley finally found Livingstone holed up near Lake Tanganyika. He walked up to the lost Scotsman and asked him the famous question, '*Dr Livingstone, I presume . . . ?*'

I don't know what the doctor replied but if I'd have been Livingstone I'd have said something along the lines of . . .

Of course I'm Dr Livingstone! Who else could I possibly be – a monkey in a hat?

Well that's what you look like to me . . .

Stanley tried to persuade him to give up his mission and return home, but the explorer refused – he was still determined to find the source of the Nile. He never did, though, and he died in Africa in 1873. After his death, Livingstone's body was brought back to Britain and buried with great ceremony in Westminster Abbey, but his heart was buried separately in Africa, the continent he loved.

ANYONE GOT A RULER?

Livingstone's expeditions brought Africa to everybody's attention. People realized that there was a lot more to the mighty continent than just jungle. For a start there were plants that produced valuable things like rubber, cotton, cocoa and palm oil. And under the ground there were precious stones like diamonds, and metals like copper, tin and . . .

Suddenly everybody was interested in Africa, and the countries of Europe all wanted a slice of it. So they got together with a big map, a pen and a ruler – and divided up the whole of Africa between them! Today if you look in an atlas, you can still see the straight lines they drew when they marked out some of the borders!

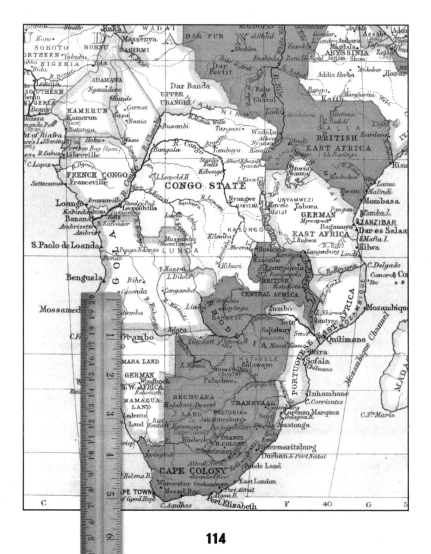

The Brits did very well out of this dividing-up business. They elbowed everyone else aside and made sure they got a huge chunk running virtually the entire length of Africa from Cairo in the North to Cape Town down in the south! At a stroke this massive piece of land became pink in all the maps of the world . . .

Pink?

Pink???

. . . although no one asked the Africans what they thought of this.

DOUBLE-DEALING AND DIAMONDS

But changing the colour of a country on a map, doesn't change it on the ground.

It doesn't give it roads, laws or a police force, and it doesn't make it rich enough to buy things. Britain's African colonies needed a leader – someone who could transform them into a valuable part of the Empire; and it got one . . . although unfortunately he was a complete crook!

WHIZZ-KID

In 1870, a spotty, wheezy teenager dressed in a school blazer got off the boat at Cape Town, South Africa. His name was Cecil Rhodes and he'd been sent from Britain to work on his brother's cotton farm in South Africa. He was a sickly child and his parents thought some fresh air in the warm African climate would do him good.

It was perfect timing – a few years earlier, diamonds had been discovered in South Africa near the town of Kimberley. Diamond fever was sweeping the country and anyone who could afford a shovel was going to Kimberley to dig for their fortune.

Before long, young Cecil had abandoned the cotton farm and joined in the rush to dig for diamonds. Not only did he manage to find a few but he turned out to be a whizz at business and started renting out mining equipment like water pumps to other miners. Unfortunately for the miners, Cecil also had slightly fewer morals than a sewer rat. He made sure that the only pumps the miners could use were his – by sabotaging everybody else's! And when he started raising the prices and the miners couldn't pay up, he took shares in their mines instead.

TAKING TEA WITH CANNIBALS

It wasn't just men who risked their lives exploring the furthest corners of the globe! One of the most fearless British explorers was a woman called Mary Henrietta Kingsley! Compared to her, men like Captain Cook and David Livingstone were girly wusses!

When she was young, Mary wasn't allowed to go to school or play with other kids! She had to stay at home looking after her sick

She may be a woman but she's harder than me!

mother. So to stop herself dying of boredom, she read hundreds of books and managed to teach herself super-complex stuff like physics, chemistry, biology, maths, Latin and German!

Eventually, when her mother died, she was free! So did she find a nice young man, marry him and settle down with two dogs, a cat and a budgerigar called Joey?

Absolutely not.

She was desperate to see the world she'd read so much about; so she packed her bags and bought a one-way ticket to the most exciting place she could think of – West Africa!

The Africans must have thought she looked pretty weird, hacking her way through the jungle dressed exactly like she would have back home, in a long black skirt, a black shawl and a black bonnet. But Mary was a born explorer and her clothes weren't quite as daft as you might think. One day she accidentally trod on an animal trap, and fell fifteen feet into a deep pit lined with 12-inch wooden spikes. But her huge skirt cushioned her fall and she survived with only a few bruises!

She was afraid of nothing and nobody. She lived with the local tribes, waded through waist-deep leech-infested swamps and paddled around in dug-out canoes, along the way capturing rare fish and insects, which she pickled in jars and sent back to the museums of England. She even found a tribe of cannibals called the Fang, who taught her how to cook snake!

Pretty soon Rhodes owned all the mines in Kimberley and was the richest man in Africa, but he wasn't satisfied with just being stinking rich. He thought that the British Empire was the best thing since sliced bread and that the British should rule the whole world. It was his duty to take as much of Africa as possible in the name of Britain. In his own words – he wanted to paint the map of Africa red from top to bottom! So he used his money to buy up all the land he could. When the local tribes refused to sell to him, he bribed, cheated, stole and threatened until they gave in. If all else failed, he sent in a load of mean-looking guys with guns to take it by force.

In 1888 Rhodes made the local king (in modern-day Zimbabwe) sign a contract giving him the rights to mine all the minerals in Matabeleland. What the king didn't know was that he was really signing away *all rights* to his land – Rhodes sent in his own private police force to take control of Matabeleland and they killed anyone who got in the way.

Large swathes of Southern Africa became part of the British Empire, and in case anyone forgot who was responsible, Rhodes had part of it named after himself – 'Rhodesia'!

With me on the stamps, everyone has to lick my . . .

SOUTHERN RHODESIA
1890 1940
CECIL JOHN RHODES
THE FOUNDER
1½

SMELLY AIR

Africa was a very dangerous place, but it wasn't the man-eating lions, poisonous snakes or angry natives that were most likely to kill you, it was the hundreds of gross tropical diseases.

It's not my fault you humans are so tasty!

West Africa was the worst – set foot there and it was only a matter of months before you broke out in a burning fever, came up in a horrible rash or turned yellow; sometimes all your fingers and toes fell off. So many Europeans died there that it was renamed the 'White Man's Grave'!

One British Governor returned from a trip to find that his local lawyer, the chief justice, his secretary and the chaplain had all dropped dead from disease! The only person still doing business was the carpenter – he was busy making coffins!

We agree – yum-yum!

Doctors didn't know what caused these diseases – some believed they came from the smelly air around the stagnant marshes (the name 'malaria' comes from the Italian for 'bad air') – and nobody had the faintest idea how to cure them.

Grace's Guide to . . .
TREATING AFRICAN DISEASES

A lot of the treatments they devised for you were worse than getting sick in the first place! Leeches were placed on your head to 'suck out' the fever . . .

. . . boiling hot cloths were slapped on your skin, causing large blisters which were then pierced to 'drain away' the illness . . .

Doctors fed you doses of mercury which made you drool a lot and caused all your hair and teeth to fall out, or made your mouth swell up until you suffocated on your own tongue . . .

Then in the 1850s, it was discovered that taking a daily dose of the drug 'quinine' (a powder made from a South American tree bark) could ward off malaria. It tasted so bitter that the British mixed it with fizzy water and gin, creating the fashionable new drink of 'gin and tonic'!

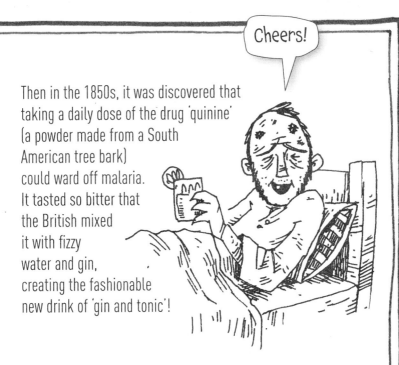

Cheers!

Medicines like quinine gave British explorers, soldiers and administrators a much better chance of survival – pretty soon they were traipsing all over West Africa claiming yet more land for the Empire!

GRACE'S TOP TEN BRITISH COLONIES

2. THE RACIST COLONY

A hundred years ago most Europeans thought that white people were better than black people. This was great if you were white, but rubbish if you were black, like most of the people living in Africa. In South Africa, which was run by the British from 1908, a law was passed saying that black people could only own 10 per cent of the country – not the good land, just the really grotty bits that nobody else wanted. Black people were also paid less than white people, got a poorer education and weren't allowed to vote. Nice, eh?

Even after South Africa left the British Empire, white South Africans carried on treating black South Africans really badly. They did everything they could to keep the blacks and the whites separate – black people couldn't use the same buses, trains, hospitals or even park benches as white people! A lot of black South Africans became rebels and fought against the whites, and people of all colours in other countries stopped buying South African goods, in order to try to make white South Africa go bust. Finally in 1990 the whites gave in and agreed to share the country with the blacks, and in 1994 South Africa got its first black president – Nelson Mandela!

President
Nelson R
Mandela

SOUTH AFRICA **45c**
SUID-AFRIKA

I was in jail for 27 years – now my face is on loads of stamps. Ain't life funny?

1. THE LAST COLONY

Britain wasn't the only Empire on the planet – the Chinese had one and theirs was over 2,000 years old. They had lots of things to sell that the British wanted to buy, like tea, silks and beautiful porcelain cups. But there was a big problem – the Chinese didn't want to let foreigners into China.

So the British took over a nearby island called Hong Kong, where their merchants could do business and, as you can imagine, the Chinese weren't very happy about that!

But there was another problem. There wasn't much that the Chinese wanted to buy from Britain, so the British did something really dodgy. They grew lots of opium (a really addictive drug that comes from poppy flowers), and smuggled it into China through Hong Kong, because they knew that if lots of Chinese people became addicted to opium they'd do anything to get it, including flogging things like tea, silks and teacups. Which makes the British Empire one of the biggest drug dealers in history! Is it any wonder the Chinese disliked us so much!

Nevertheless, Hong Kong became a thriving marketplace and one of the richest cities in the world, and Britain held on to it for as long as possible. In fact it wasn't handed back to the Chinese until 1997!

THE RISE AND FALL OF AN EMPIRE

Eventually Britain had the biggest Empire in the world . . .

in the whole of history . . .

Ever!

It was bigger than me!

Britain even had a special postage stamp with a map of the Empire on it, and the words '*We hold a vaster Empire than has ever been!*'

You could say the British were being just the teensiest bit smug.

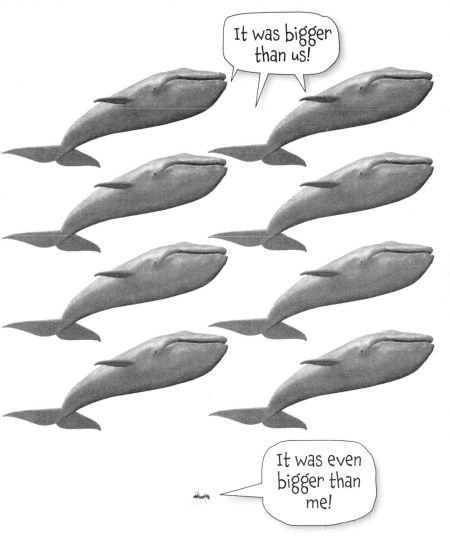

For most Brits, life without an Empire would have been very dull indeed. They loved hearing about all the exciting, colourful and dangerous things going on there. They sang songs about it, read books about it and watched films about it. They particularly enjoyed hearing about their favourite British heroes doing brave deeds and winning battles in faraway parts of it.

COOL BRITANNIA

The symbol of this mighty Empire was a large lady with a metal hat and big boobs. She'd been around for a couple of thousand years, but she was very different from how she'd originally looked.

In ancient times the Romans had thought the Britons were a feisty bunch, so their symbol for Britain had been a young woman dressed as a warrior in a Roman-style helmet and carrying a shield.

As the centuries went by, the Brits changed her a bit. They called her Britannia, gave her a three-pronged fishing spear called a trident and portrayed her standing in the sea to show everyone that now Britain had lots of fast ships, Britannia ruled the waves.

As the British Empire grew, so did Britannia. Now her shield was decorated with the British flag, and a large lion appeared by her side (because the lion was the king – or queen – of the jungle, just like the British ruler was the king or queen of the Empire).

Finally Britannia became a brand, bigger even than Adidas, Apple and Nintendo put together. Trains and ships were named after her, she appeared in magazines and newspapers, in adverts and on packets of tea, bars of soap, tins of cocoa and boxes of chocolates all over the world.

PLAY THE GAME!

One such British hero was Colonel Robert Baden-Powell. In 1899 'BP', as he was known to his mates, was ordered to defend the little South African town of Mafeking from attack by the Boers.

The Boers were Dutch settlers living in South Africa. The Brits had taken a lot of land from them, including Mafeking, and they were very unhappy about it.

For more than seven months the Boers attacked the town, trying to force Baden-Powell to surrender. But BP refused to back down, even though life was pretty tough for him and the rest of the British trapped inside. To keep spirits up he got the Boers to agree not to fight on Sundays, and instead everyone in the town joined in cricket and football matches, dances, concerts and competitions to find 'the best siege baby' and 'the finest cow in town'!

Can I play?

At one point the Boers asked if they could join in too, but BP sent back a message saying no, not until they'd finished the present match (meaning not until the fight was over). He said that the British had scored '200 days not out' and were having a 'very enjoyable game'!

But most of the Brits weren't having a 'very enjoyable game' at all. They were running out of food, and the situation got desperate. Typically, BP wasn't downhearted. He made sure that everything that could be used *was* used, and everything that could be eaten *was* eaten.

HOW TO RECYCLE A DEAD HORSE
by Robert Baden-Powell

Warning – you may need a sickbag!

1 Cut off the horse's mane and tail and send them to the hospital to stuff the pillows and mattresses.

2 Prise off its shoes, melt them, and turn them into bullets.

3 Remove its skin, head and feet, boil them up, then squeeze the whole lot into a loaf shape. Call it horse pâté and serve it on toast.

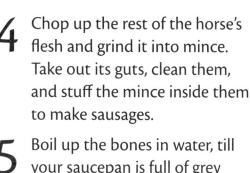

4 Chop up the rest of the horse's flesh and grind it into mince. Take out its guts, clean them, and stuff the mince inside them to make sausages.

5 Boil up the bones in water, till your saucepan is full of grey gloop, then throw in a few vegetables and turn it into soup.

Don't try this at home, children!

BADEN – POWELL'S TUCK SHOP

PÂTÉ & TOAST
with horse

SOUP
with horse

SAUSAGES
with horse

FLOUR
with horse

FLOUR

6 Dry the bones, grind them into powder, then mix them into your sacks of baking flour to make it go further.

Wait till the next horse dies, then start again.

Eventually, extra British troops were sent to help the besieged forces – the Boers were defeated and Baden-Powell was announced the winner! (Britain – 1; The Boers – 0.) Hurrah!

BEING PREPARED

There weren't enough soldiers at Mafeking, so BP recruited local boys to do various army jobs, like acting as messengers and lookouts, and cycling round the town delivering messages while dodging enemy bullets (I bet that made them pedal fast!). He called this gang of lads the 'Mafeking Cadet Corps'.

If you made kids do this sort of thing nowadays, people would say it was cruelty to children, but Baden-Powell believed it was good for them because it toughened them up. He thought every young boy (and girl) should be prepared to do their duty for the Empire. In fact he got so excited about this that when he got back home to England, he started the Boy Scouts, and dressed them up just like the Mafeking Cadet Corps in big hats, shorts and khaki uniforms.

He wrote a book called *Scouting for Boys* full of all the things he thought boys ought to know, like how to tie knots, light fires, stalk deer and make a camp. It also contained useful advice on how to save somebody from drowning, stop a runaway horse, survive being run over by a train and control a mad dog.

Lots of British kids thought all this sounded like great fun and by the end of 1908 more than 60,000 boys had signed up to become Scouts! Two years later the Guides were formed so that girls could join in too.

THE ANGRY MAN

Britain wasn't the only country that wanted to rule the world. By 1914 Germany was just like Britain. It had lots of money and people and factories. It also had its own mini-Empire in Asia and Africa.

This made everybody in Britain very nervous. They didn't like the idea of the Germans becoming more powerful than them, and it wasn't long before the two Empires got into a serious fight. It became the biggest war the world had ever known, and it was called . . . **World War One**.

. . . although obviously people who fought in it didn't call it World War One, because they didn't know there was going to be a World War Two.

yeah yeah, clever-clogs! They called it the Great War, or the War to end all wars . . .

It was called a 'World War' because it wasn't just fought by Britain and Germany – it was Britain *and* all her colonies v. Germany *and* all her colonies, *plus* all the other countries of Europe who joined in on one side or the other, *plus* all their colonies.

In other words . . . pretty much the whole world.

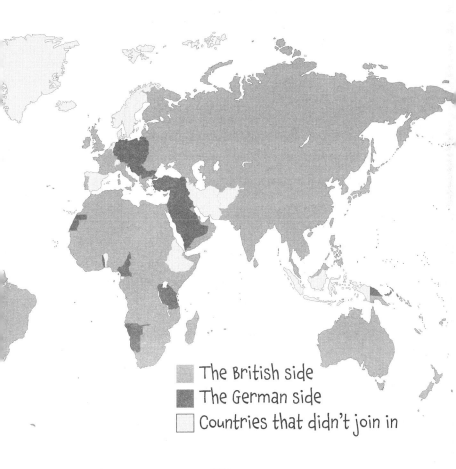

The British side
The German side
Countries that didn't join in

This was a very different kind of war from the ones Britain had been used to fighting in her Empire. Those usually involved British soldiers with machine guns duffing up a bunch of locals with pointed sticks. But the Germans had the same kind of technologies as Britain,

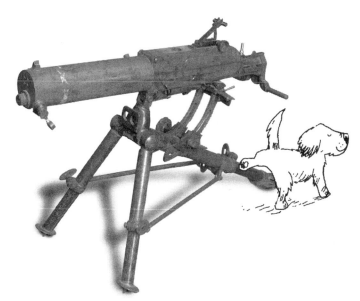

and could make things like boats, trains, high explosives and submarines, as well as lots and lots of machine guns. Which made beating them much harder.

For four years, both sides slogged it out on battlefields all around the globe. War was a lot less fun when you couldn't just pop over to a foreign country and wipe out the enemy because you'd got a few soldiers who were armed to the teeth. Instead battles now lasted months or even years, with everybody fighting in the swampy gaps between rows of muddy trenches and the barbed wire.

Millions died and most people were very glad when it was over (even the Germans, who lost) . . .

But then, twenty years later, Germany and Britain had another big row. By now Germany was led by an angry man with a little moustache called Adolf Hitler.

HELLO, HITLER!

Adolf Hitler was the leader of a bunch of Germans called the Nazi Party. Nazis liked dressing up in uniform, doing a silly straight-legged walk called the 'goose-step', and sticking their right arm in the air while shouting 'Heil Hitler' (which means 'Hello, Hitler' in German, but not in a friendly way).

They hated anyone who was a bit different from them. This included Jewish people, gypsies, foreigners, people with dark skin, people with sticky-up hair, in fact anyone who wasn't blond-haired, blue-eyed and shouted 'Heil Hitler!' while doing a funny walk.

Interestingly, Hitler didn't have blond hair or blue eyes (he wasn't even German, he was actually from Austria), but nobody seemed too keen to point this out.

I shall rule the world!

He doesn't half go on.

Hitler was angry about a lot of things (he was angry that he wasn't blond-haired and blue eyed for a start), but mostly he was angry that Germany hadn't won World War One. He thought Germany should be running the world by now – not Britain.

He was so angry that he decided to start another war – and this time he was determined that Germany would win it and he would rule the world!!!

So Germany and Britain went to war (again) . . .

Plus all Britain's colonies (again) . . .

Plus all the other major countries in the world (again), who all joined one side or the other (again) . . .

In other words, welcome to World War Two.

I hope this turns out better than last time . . .

Millions of people from all over the Empire fought on the same side as the British. They came from places like Canada, India, Australia, Africa and the Caribbean, as well as from other European countries like France, Poland and Norway. But the German side was stronger, and Britain and her allies were soon losing big-time.

Then the Russians decided to fight alongside the Allies . . . Hooray!

And the Japanese joined Hitler's side . . . Boo!

But then finally good-old, gun-toting, Stetson-wearing, movie-making, McDonald's-eating, freedom-loving US of A (or America for short) joined the Allied side!!!!

AMERICA JOINS IN

The Americans didn't like the British Empire – they thought countries should be free to run their own affairs and shouldn't have to do what the bossy Brits told them. But they liked Hitler even less. So they agreed to help the Allies win the war by lending them money and weapons and sending American soldiers to fight alongside them. This was the big turning point in the war. There was still a lot more fighting to be done, and millions more people died, but eventually Britain, America, Russia and the rest of the Allies won and Germany lost (again).

THE EMPIRE GOES BROKE

You'd think that having won two World Wars the British Empire would now be greater than ever! But it wasn't. It was broke.

All those guns, bombs, boats, submarines and planes had cost billions of pounds. Britain had spent all its money winning the war and couldn't afford to run an Empire any more. To make things worse, more and more people around the Empire were complaining that they wanted to be free to do their own thing.

One of the first people to make a big fuss about this were the Indians, led by a man called Gandhi who wore spectacles and a loincloth.

SOUL FORCE!

Mohandas Gandhi was an Indian lawyer who wanted to show everyone that poor people were just as smart and just as important as the rich, so he gave away all his possessions and his expensive clothes! From then on he lived as simply as the very poorest people in India (who were very, very poor indeed!).

Gandhi believed that the lives of ordinary Indians would be better if they were free – which meant no longer having to be part of the British Empire. But instead of fighting the British to make them leave, he used what he called 'soul force'. This meant encouraging Indians to disobey British rules and laws but without using violence.

The rules for using 'soul force' included:

Don't Get Angry

Don't Insult Your Enemy

Don't Use Violence Against Your Enemy

Sounds mad, doesn't it? But it worked! The British got really annoyed at Gandhi and his followers because they wouldn't do what they were told. But what made this even more infuriating was that, whenever the Brits tried to force the Indians to do something, it was the Brits who ended up looking really bad.

Gandhi's 'soul force' eventually paid off big-time. In 1947, after World War Two had been won, Britain gave in, divided the country in two (calling one part Pakistan while the other half kept the name India), and gave the two new countries their independence.

END OF THE EMPIRE

After India, lots of other countries around the Empire started demanding that Britain shove off and leave them to it.

Britain quickly backed down and one by one each country won its independence. They were now free to have their own government and make their own rules.

It wasn't going to be easy – in many places the British had run everything for years and nobody else knew how to do it. If they didn't learn pretty fast, their whole country might collapse!

But at least it was now up to them – and they didn't have to sing a nonsense song any more about a queen they'd never met who lived on a cold little island thousands of miles away.

Here are ALL the countries that were once part of the British Empire. Protectorates meant a country would pay for Britain's protection and advice. Mandates were international agreements. The bold countries are STILL British – they're called the British Overseas Territories.

NAME	COLONY	INDEPENDENCE	NOW CALLED
Aden	1858	1967	Yemen
American Colonies (various)	From 1622	1783	USA
Anguilla	**1663**		
Antigua	1663	1981	
Ascension	**1815**		
Australian colonies (various)	From 1803	1942	
Bahamas	1717	1973	
Bahrain	1835 (Protectorate)	1971	
Baluchistan	1877	1947	Pakistan
Barbados	1627	1966	
Barbuda	1628	1981	
Basutoland	1868	1966	Lesotho
Bay Islands	1742	1860 to Honduras	
Bechuanaland	1885 (Protectorate)	1966	Botswana
Bermuda	**1684**		
Bhutan	1911 (Protectorate)	1947	
British Cameroons	1914	1961	Nigeria/Cameroon
British Guiana	1815	1966	Guyana
British Honduras	1786	1981	Belize
British Indian Ocean Territory	**1784**		
British New Guinea	1886	1975	Papua New Guinea
British Somaliland	1905	1960	Somalia
British Virgin Islands	**1786**		
Brunei	1888 (Protectorate)	1983	
Burma	1824	1948	
Canadian colonies (various)	From 1763	1982	
Cayman Islands	**1670**		
Ceylon	1796	1948	Sri Lanka
Christmas Island (Pacific)	1888	1979	
Cyprus*	1914	1960	
Dominica	1763	1978	
Egypt	1882	1954	
Eire/Ireland	1801 (part of UK)	1935	
Ellice Islands	1916	1978	Tuvalu
Eritrea	1941	1952	
Falkland Islands	**1841**		
Fiji	1874	1970	
Gambia	1821	1965	
Gibraltar	**1704**		
Gilbert Islands	1916	1979	Kiribati

* There are two large military bases on Cyprus that are also still parts of Britain.

Gold Coast	1821	1957	Ghana
Grenada	1763	1974	
Hawaii	1843	1893 to USA	
Hong Kong	1842	1997 to China	
Indian colonies (various)	From 1620	1947	
Ionian Islands	1809	1864 to Greece	
Jamaica	1655	1962	
Kenya	1920	1963	
Kuwait	1899 (Protectorate)	1961	
Malaya	1874 (Protectorate)	1957	Malaysia
Maldive Islands	1887 (Protectorate)	1965	
Malta	1800	1964	
Mauritius	1810	1968	
Minorca	1708	1803 to Spain	
Montserrat	**1663**		
Mosquito Coast	1655 (Protectorate)	1860	Honduras/Nicaragua
Nepal	1816 (Protectorate)	1947	
Newfoundland	1497	1949 to Canada	
New Hebrides	1906	1980	Vanuatu
New Zealand	1769	1947	
Nigeria	1914	1960	
North Borneo	1881 (Protectorate)	1963 to Malaysia	
Northern Rhodesia	1924	1964	Zambia
Nyasaland	1907	1964	Malawi
Oman	1800 (Protectorate)	1970	
Palestine	1920 (Mandate)	1948	
Penang	1826 (Protectorate)	1957	Malaysia
Pitcairn Island	**1838**		
Qatar	1916 (Protectorate)	1971	
Roanoke	1585-1587?		
St Christopher	1663	1983	St Kitts and Nevis
St Helena	**1834**		
St Lucia	1778	1979	
St Vincent	1762	1979	
Samoa	1899	1962	
Sarawak	1946	1963	Malaysia
Seychelles	1794	1976	
Sierra Leone	1807	1961	
Singapore	1826 (Protectorate)	1965	
Solomon Islands	1893 (Protectorate)	1978	
South Africa	1910	1934	
South Georgia	**1775**		
Southern Rhodesia	1890	1980	Zimbabwe
Sudan	1898	1956	
Suez Canal Zone	1881	1956	Egypt
Swaziland	1893 (Protectorate)	1963	
Tanganyika	1919 (Mandate)	1961	Tanzania
Tonga	1879 (Protectorate)	1970	
Transjordan	1920 (Mandate)	1946	Jordan
Transvaal	1877	1910 to South Africa	
Trinidad and Tobago	1762	1962	
Tristan da Cunha	**1816**		
Trucial Oman	1892 (Protectorate)	1971	United Arab Emirates
Turks and Caicos Islands	**1766**		
Uganda	1905	1962	
Zanzibar	1890 (Protectorate)	1963	Tanzania

TIMELINE

1492   Christopher Columbus sails off from Spain to sneak up on the East . . . by sailing west!

1497   John Cabot gets to Newfoundland and finds it's flooded with fish

1581   Francis Drake gets made a 'Sir'

1587   The British colonists of Roanoke, America, vanish into thin air

1588   The King of Spain sends an Armada of ships to attack England

1603   Queen Elizabeth dies, and King James takes over

1607   Enterprising Brits head to Virginia to grow tobacco

1642   The Civil Wars begin in England

1655   The British swipe Jamaica from the Spanish

1666   The Great Fire of London

1704   The British swipe Gibraltar from the Spanish

1707   England and Scotland join up into a Union

1769   The first British people land in New Zealand

1769   James Watt invents a new and improved steam engine, which will power all sorts of new industries for Britain

1770s   James Cook leads a naval expedition to explore the Pacific, and discovers Australia

1776   America declares its independence from Britain – Britain takes a few years to get used to the idea

1783   Britain recognizes the independence of its American colonies

1801   Act of Union creates the 'United Kingdom of Great Britain and Ireland'

1804	Richard Trevithick shows off his railway 'steam horse'
1805	Napoleon and a huge fleet try to bash the British. Lord Nelson stops him at the Battle of Trafalgar, but dies in the process
1807	The British government bans selling or buying slaves
1830	The Liverpool and Manchester Railway opens; William Huskisson becomes the first man to be killed by a train
1837	Victoria becomes Queen of England
1840	David Livingstone heads for Africa
1838	The SS *Great Western* makes the first steam-powered trip across the Atlantic
1839	The First Opium War between Britain and China begins
1845	The Potato Famine begins in Ireland
1851	The Great Exhibition opens in the shiny new Crystal Palace
1857	The Indian Mutiny
1858	The British government takes over India from the East India Company
1861	Prince Albert dies, and Victoria starts wearing black
1870	A telegraph cable is laid all the way from Britain to India
1876	Queen Victoria of Great Britain gets a promotion, and becomes Empress of India too!
1879	The Brits invade Zululand in Southern Africa
1892	Mary Kingsley sets off on her travels
1899	Britain fights the Boers over who gets to rule South Africa
1901	Queen Victoria dies
1914–1918	World War One
1922	Southern Ireland gets independence from Britain as the 'Irish Free State'
1939–1945	World War Two
1947	India and Pakistan become independent from Britain

QUIZ

1 Who did the Spanish call 'The Dragon'?

2 Which English king first decided he should be king of Ireland too?

3 Who found buckets and buckets of cod in Newfoundland?

4 Which of these things did you have to be to join the Royal Navy?
  • willing
  • able to swim
  • a man

5 What new trend did Queen Victoria's son Edward sport?

6 How many tails did a ship's 'cat' have?

7 What did Nelson's friends use to stop his dead body from rotting?

8 Where did Richard Trevithick want to go in his new steam train?

9 How fast was Stephenson's Rocket?

10 How many passengers travelled to America on the *Great Western*'s first voyage?

11 Which invention was the Victorian 't-mail'?

12 What did Queen Victoria call the happiest day of her life?

13 What did Lieutenant Halkett's ingenious rubber coat transform into?

14 Why did Captain Waterman have to crawl through a sewer to get out of the governor's house in Lucknow?

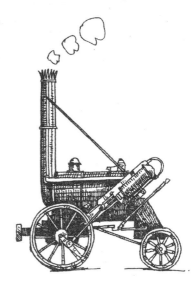

15 What did Richard Burton do when someone laughed at his moustache?

16 What was Victoria Falls called, before Victoria ever heard of it?

17 What saved Mary Kingsley's life when she fell into a spiky pit?

Tony Robinson's Weird World of Wonders is a multi-platform extravaganza (which doesn't mean it's a circus in a large railway station). You can get my World of Wonders game on line, there's a website, ebook, audio versions, extra stories and bits of weirdly wonderful design, marketing and publicity. In order to get all those things sorted out, I've surrounded myself with a grown-up version of the Curiosity Crew. They are Dan Newman (Design), Amy Lines (Marketing), Sally Oliphant (Publicity), James Luscombe (Digital), Tom Skipp (Ebooks), and Becky Lloyd (Audio). A big thanks to them all; they are committed, funny and extremely cool.

Tony has to say that otherwise they'd stop work and go home!

Also available in this series

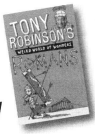

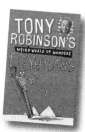